Last thing you should read, if it comes to that.

Tanushree kagayaku

BookLeaf
Publishing

Presentation by *BookLeaf Publishing*

Web: www.bookleafpub.com

E-mail: info@bookleafpub.com

ISBN: 978-93-95314-23-7

First edition 2022

DEDICATION

To all the elements that confluenced despair,
not forever but, again and again and again,

ACKNOWLEDGEMENT

A shout out goes to everyone I have interacted with for a passing moment or for hours over years. To name; my father, mother and brother for being by my side through all the ups and downs.

Rejoicing flame of light

She is the candle
He struck the match
Out came a bright
Rejoicing flame of light

He gave me the base
She helped me fly
He gave me the firm foothold
She gave me wings to fly

Her hand was there
We could talk
I was also talking to him
In my head, though

She knew what she meant
Never told him what he meant
He probably knows
Maybe not
She appreciates it
So does he

Had my ups and downs with him
That's when she held my hand
But let's not forget he was the one
Who put my hand in her hand

I am tempted to say
He and she
My parents, not by blood.
But parents have their place.
They have their restraints, their fights
They have their place in my world
Our different relationship
Different roles to play

This is in a sense freer
More pure more meaningful
This is not because it had to
Because it wants to

The front for the world

Natively from the desert, she speaks five
languages.
Notably, she thinks in her mother tongue –
Kutchi,
spoken by barely a million on the planet.
And so, she makes all of existence her family.
Being around multiple generations at home,
Loved & inspired by an elder sibling,
She proudly wears her badge of bisexuality,
Carrying the torch of gender fluidity in women.
Brought up in a Jain family,

She watches first-hand the difficulty yet
criticality,
Of practicing non-violence in thought and
action.
So she earnestly treads the path of righteousness.
Consciously seeing the vitality of mental health
today,
She practices Vipassana (meditation) and
Yogasana
Hoping she can light up her own day and
others'.
With glee, she makes a mess with canvas &
paints,

Plays kho-kho in the dirt,
Reads science by day and literature at bedtime.
Dabbling in Kathak, Kuchipudi, Salsa, and pole
dancing,
She revels in people's company, yet finds solace
in solitude.

An abstract artist & topologist,
Her visual intuition and analytic mindset

Creates a universe of strange ideas that words
cannot describe,

So she paints the nights away,
Her thoughts naked in the colors for all to see.
She sits by the curbside in delight,
Chatting with artists and local historians,
Dreamily learning about art historical trends.
The past has so much to offer!
Rich stories and movements call out to her,
And giving in to the forces of mythology, art,
and philosophy
She has been a museum guide and a history buff
Navigating people through the ancient
intersection between the three.

Traveling solo with gusto, she embraces cultures
with naivety
Longing to see Antarctica and the rawness of
our planet,
She has resolved to reward herself with a trip.
Just has to complete her research!
Math, and teaching its tenets,
Brings about a fervor in her
Sharing her knowledge & ideas with
students,
She engages enthusiasts in America, and across
Europe & Asia.
Humbled by her learnings and observations,
She strives to remove all constraints as she
teaches.
The classroom rewards her openness,
Thought-provoking ideas & discussions
with her students,

Which brings a smile to her face

As she recreates her inclusive childhood all over
again.

With the ardent belief
That Math can be exciting for everyone,
She actively engages the quiet, the meek, the
underdogs,
And helps to give them a fighting chance.
Using the long reach of the Internet and social
platforms,
She searches for the gems, the diamonds in the
rough
To spread her love of math beyond the borders
of the privileged.

The hypnotist

The class I couldn't bunk,
The love I couldn't hide.
The eyes I can't meet,
The crush who didn't propose.
The colors we splashed,
The dinners we had,
The laughs we had,
The days we spend.
The class he will take,
The project we will do.
The discussion we'll have,
The company I'll enjoy.
The math I have to do,
The motivation he'll give,
The distraction he'll become.
The books I will read,
The path I will weave,
The guidance he'll give.
The fantasy I have, of
The knots he will tie,
The strap he'll undo,
The things I'll lose.
The respect I have,
The memories I have,
Will all I have,

That is all I need.
The love I got,
The passion I saw,
I lay on my bed,
Thinking of the days ahead.

The question

What are you Jealous of?
Looking in the mirror,
I ask myself one day.

If someone worked hard for it,
They have earned it.
You can too.

If someone, had it by virtue of birth,
They haven't really earned it.
Although you can cultivate and earn it.

So, What are you jealous of?

The answer

Settler is not me
Reacher, my love
Has Jealousy.

Stagnant is not me
Growth, my friend
Has Jealousy.

Look for the good in people
Don't be a pessimist, my outlook
Has Jealousy

Don't be so harsh on yourself
But I aim to
Have Jealousy over myself.

To senior, from OfHarshad

The first time we met,
There was a passing infatuation.
6 years later,
A casual chat
And a promised call.
Still casual
You pick up the call and
SAY Hello Tanushree
My mouth's dry
Words don't come out
I am sweating
I reach out for Sorbitrate
Only to realize it was kcatta traeh.

Instantaneous comfort
But still not close friends
Too assumptive of you
My heart sank
Too scared to offend you again
I take my clawing paw back

My mind is filled with what-ifs
He's curious but still distant
He'll open up
Give him time, I told myself.

I came off as a socially sorted creature
But truth be told I was as nervous.
I said I can confess my feelings
That's far from the truth
It's better to keep secrets, you said.
Better tell than regret, I roared but like a kitten.
It's such a good feeling to know someone likes
you, you said creating a tornado in my little
kitten head
Nonetheless, I pour my heart out,
Not on the call but here.

Should I send him or not?
Wait till we have our next call
What if he is busy?
What if he doesn't like it?
What if it's too much?
He's my senior, what if he's annoyed, frustrated,
or worse angry?
Will he punish me?
I pull myself out of dreams
To realize this is the reality

The bp machine fails to give me a reading
As I send this out to you
Should switch off my phone?
At least switch off the internet

The cursor blinking
Waiting for my action
I am incapacitated
Senior had asked me to sleep
Disobeying him, I wrote him a poem
What will he do?
Give me a call?
He might think that I am sleeping
But sleep alludes to me
What will I say if he does?
Yes senior
Yeah, that is what I'll say
What if punishes me,
For being upfront, for disobeying, for ...
I'll take it. I'll take whatever he must lash out.

The waiting

I sent it out to him
Not thinking much
Could not think much
The rain pouring outside

Should I delete it?
We are not that close you had said
This was a mistake
I regret it now

I close my eyes
Try to sleep
Can't cry can't sleep
Why do these feelings have to be this strong
I can do with a milder version

Patience, patience, patience
Breath in breath out hold, repeat
Yash, Yash, Yash
I can't call him that
Senior, m sorry
Clumsy cloud of thoughts
All my rejections hit me in the head
You, little pixie head

Twisting in bed
I think
It's not the punishment he'll give
Waiting, itself is my punishment.

The way out

Obsession about that thing
The only way out
Is getting completely in
Live it to the fullest
Give yourself enough dose.

Then comes the other thing to be obsessed with.

Obsessed about a person
The only way out
Is get them completely in
Live with them to the fullest
Never give them enough.

But can you really be patient to not give away
your whole self?

In it again

I go about my day
As usual, as I can.
His thoughts linger in my mind
Can't get him out

That troubles me
I don't know exactly what.
The only way to be sane is
To keep working
To be continuously distracted

Why do I even want to talk with him?
Meet him? Need his validation?
Don't think of the why, I tell myself

I can't move on.
He texts sometimes.
And I hang by that thread.

Don't text him
Don't text him
Don't text him
That is my mantra.

Reply only if he asks you to.
Be cool.
This isn't love.
It's just a desperate need for approval.

You are enough for yourself
Your approval is enough
You are secure with yourself
And you are good enough for yourself.

I keep telling myself
In desperate need to get out of mind
But he still lingers
But it's fine.

Losing myself

I am not an artist
I am not a viewer
I am not a muse
I am not a girl
I am not a daughter
I am not a sister
I am not a wife
I am not a girlfriend
I am not a lover
I am not a mathematician
I am not a dancer
I am not a student
I am not a teacher
I am not a reader
I am not a writer
I am not a speaker
I am not a listener
I am not an existentialist
I am not an absurdist
I am not a nihilist
I am not a scientist
I am not a traveler
I am not an extrovert
I am not an introvert
I am not a chaotic monkey

I am not a flowing stream
I am not a loner
I am not a chit chatter
I am not a millennial
I am not a Gen-Z

I am not insecure
I am not vulnerable
I am not anxious
I am not scared
I am not depressed

I am none of those
But I am all of those
And more
I am an experience
I am the interaction.

Getting back the grip

If nobody writes it
And nobody reads
Is that book
Still a book?

If nobody made it
And nobody has seen it
Is that art
Still an art?

If nobody gives you a hand
And nobody sees through you
Are you,
Still yourself?

If nobody pushes you
And nobody validates you
Are you any less,
Or still yourself?

Slipped on the way up

Loved a night
Hated over the next day
Then You did not matter
In any which way.

He read it, didn't get it!

The gift of
The secret packet of cigarettes. In
The hope that
The agony ends sooner than later.

...It continues

She's crazy, half of me
Can't do a lot about it,
How much ever I hate her
Imagine killing her, but
There's evolution ruining my plan.
Not enough options to work around

Increasing your tolerance
is what I am told of.
Doesn't tolerance shut down the rebel?
What if Gandhi was tolerant?
Your own hero, what if?

If I think back, she herself was a rebel.
Is she trying to save me the agony?
Is she saving me the effort of,
the path she's already traversed?
Could be. She wishes well, I know.

Knowing that makes it a little more tolerable.
But that's not a solution.
But I also know, there is no solution.
This is a process every generation goes through.

A fight I have as a daughter today,
Will turn tables in the next 20 years
I'll be in my mother's shoes
And that's how it continues.

I just hope I do a better job.
Cause she'll be even crazier than me.
I'll have lesser time
But more support.
I hope I don't pass my insecurities down
But what can I say, I am just another human in
town!

Trying different perspective

…Housewife with a
Common husband.
Wattle necked aunt with
Large grey-headed uncle.
Pied piper followed by
Waging kids.
Roller boy skating past, the
Babbling girl.
Whistling roadside Romeo
Staring at the sunbird in a bikini.
Painted drag queen, with
Bronze wig cabaret.
Black legginged dancer, with
White-throated singer.
Laughing Gabbar, the villain &
Spotted Cruella, the vamp.
Short-toed hero &
White-breasted heroin, with
Orange-collared comedian.

The bird-watching it all,
In the movie staring…

Some wisdom

Thank you
for bringing me closer to my family
Now I know, they'll be always there

Thank you
For Breaking me down
Now I have met a stronger me.

Thank you
For shattering my golden glasses
Now I am prepared for life's woes and whimsy.

Thank you
For snatching my protective coat
Nothing makes me anxious now

Thank you
For bringing me one step closer to reality
Now I can appreciate my life better

Thank you
For not respecting my dignity
Now my sense of self-respect is reached its
pinnacle.

Thank you
For shattering my identity
Now I have built a better one.

Some acceptance

Sometimes you hide the inner child from the
world around
To protect it
But how long will you be strong?
Where do you go?
When your shoulders hurt,
When the pressure is above your head,
When you want to put your guards down
Where do you go?

It needs a safe space to come out then
You yourself are that space
Be with yourself
Give yourself that space
That freedom
Date yourself
Converse with self-image and self-confidence

Systematic behavior identities

Being slapped is
Being cared for.
Given your space
You don't matter.

This is the Indian school system.

It's either scolding you
Or the silent treatment.
One makes you angry
The other dejecting.

This is the Indian parenting system.

Can there be a different path,
a middle ground,
a balanced version,
motivating but not disappointing,
I wonder?

Independent or All alone

The girl who looked up to the giant
To take her in his palms
To be cared for
Instead, he walked over her
Ignoring her
Crushing her forever.

The girl had put him on the giant pedestal
As she took it away
the crushing didn't hurt.

But the pedestal had a vacuum now.

The urgency to fill it
Gave her a panic attack.

Looked all around
Under and above,
Back and forth,
but the search continued.

Tired she sat down
On the pedestal.

Chance meeting; it giveth and taketh away

Was looking for big answers
For the world's big problems
From the learned old man
Got it in his child's smile.
The validation of mentoring him
Gave grounding to my existence.
His excitement to fight
I teach him to give out controlled blows.
My impulsive mind
My uncle taught me to grout it.
Mentor mentee
Cycle continues.

Reassurance

Sometimes I wish you could take away
everything from me
Body, Mind, and Soul said slave squirming in
existential crisis.
That means you are free, and we can't have that,
Can we? Replied master reassuring her.

Sometimes I wish you could take away
everything from me
Body, Mind, and Soul said slave squirming in
existential crisis.
Nothing is yours,
for me to take away, replied master reassuring
her.

Sometimes I wish you could take away
everything from me
Body, Mind, and Soul said slave squirming in
existential crisis.
There is no Body, Mind, or Soul.
There is no you, replied master reassuring her.